THE DIGITAL UNDERGRAD

Surviving and Thriving in the Online Education Universe

College and High School Workbook

VICTORIA BARRETT

SUGARCUBE EDITING AND PUBLISHING
INDIANAPOLIS

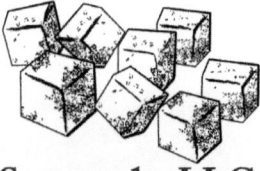

Sugarcube LLC
Indianapolis, IN
sugarcubewritingandediting.com

Parents' Workbook, Digital Undergrad Notebooks, and other goodies available at digitalundergrad.com.

ISBN: 978-1-7354544-7-4

CONTENTS

INTRODUCTION: WELL, WHAT DO WE HAVE HERE?   5

GET IT TOGETHER   15

   YOUR DIGITAL CLASSROOM   17

   YOUR DIGITAL WORKDAY   23

   ORGANIZING YOUR COURSES   29

EVERY DAY   33

   COMMUNICATION STRATEGIES   35

   READING ONLINE   47

   ACTIVE LEARNING   53

TOOLS & RESOURCES   57

   LIST OF TEMPLATES AND GUIDES   59

   YOUR PERFECT WORKSPACE: STUFF YOU NEED   61

   YOUR PERFECT WORKSPACE:

      STUFF YOU DON'T NEED   62

CALCULATING YOUR WORK TIME 63

DAILY ONLINE STUDY SCHEDULE 65

WEEKLY ONLINE STUDY SCHEDULE 66

PROJECT/TOPIC/UNIT COURSE ORGANIZATION 67

EXAM-BASED COURSE ORGANIZATION 68

WEEKLY CALENDAR COURSE ORGANIZATION 69

UNDERSTANDING ASSIGNMENTS WORKSHEET 70

LECTURE NOTES TEMPLATE 71

VIDEO/STREAMING SESSION NOTES TEMPLATE 72

READING ASSIGNMENT NOTES TEMPLATE 73

COMMUNICATION: EMAIL CHECKLIST 74

COMMUNICATION: GROUP CHAT POST CHECKLIST 75

COMMUNICATION: DISCUSSION POST CHECKLIST 76

ASSIGNMENT CHECKLIST: BEFORE YOU SUBMIT 77

ORGANIZATION: APPS, SITES, AND LOGINS LIST 78

ADDITIONAL NOTES 79

WELL, WHAT DO WE HAVE HERE?

Classes. On computers.

The promise of online learning is huge: anyone with a computer and internet access can learn, no matter where. No walls, no limitations.

The reality is a little different.

Online learning can be liberating, flexible, inventive, and welcoming. But for more students than not, it is none of those things. In fact, in college programs, roughly half of the students who enroll in online classes don't complete their courses with passing grades (though statistics vary widely among programs and schools). And those are students who *choose* online classes. In an emergency like the coronavirus pandemic of 2020, when students from preschool to PhD are forced into online learning, success rates are likely to be even lower.

What gives? Are online classes harder than "normal" ones? Are they so much easier that students lose interest?

No and no.

In the many years I've taught college freshmen in every learning context—in classrooms, online, and in hybrids that combine the two—one quality has overwhelmingly determined student success: Engagement. Students who stay engaged with their courses, who do all the work and communicate clearly and frequently with their instructors, pass, and often exceed their own expectations. Those who fall out of good habits face much more difficulty.

Online learning amplifies the challenges to student engagement. Screens are distracting. Email, discussion board, and chat communication is difficult without the advantages of body language and verbal tone. Courses are designed in ways that don't conform to our expectations, or ask us to use technologies and learning styles we are not accustomed to or comfortable with. Those challenges are amplified further when we take more than one online course at a time: instructors design courses in the best way they can manage for their disciplines, but not necessarily in ways that overlap conveniently. And many instructors, while they have the very best intentions, are not as effective at online course design as they are in the classroom.

What to do? The simple answer is to avoid online education, which might work in a perfect world. But even in the case where we we *can* choose to avoid online classes, doing so might limit options. Students love that online courses allow them to work more shifts during school, to participate in activities that might conflict with scheduled class meetings, and to learn on a schedule that suits their needs for rest and productivity. But perhaps more importantly, students can continue their education during periods of crisis, illness, or disability when courses are offered online.

There's a better way. Developing the skills to stay engaged in coursework opens up the opportunities online education offers while minimizing its disadvantages. This workbook will prepare you to do just that, whether you're choosing to take a single online course, pursuing a fully online program, or shifting into emergency-online-learning in a panic.

Getting control of five elements of your online education will help you succeed: expectations, organization, time management, study skills, and resourcefulness.

Write down 3 things you love, or expect to love, if you're new to this, about online classes:

1. _____

_____

2. _____

_____

3. _____

_____

Write down three things you hate about online classes:

1. _____

_____

2. _____

_____

3. _____

_____

EXPECTATIONS

Smart students know that online classwork should be just as difficult (or easy) as in-person classes. This is what you want as a student: easier classwork means you don't learn as much in a course; too much challenge monopolizes your time. While everyone wants completed credits and good grades, your classwork should be about learning skills and information that prepares you for future courses and, eventually, your life's work. Students who expect to be challenged in their online coursework are more often ready to succeed.

Unfortunately, many students expect online classes to be easier than "regular" classes. Those students come into their courses poorly prepared to meet their instructors' expectations. They're not ready to excel in their coursework *or* to overcome the additional challenges of the online learning environment.

Likewise, students can't expect their instructors to conduct online courses in a uniform way, or in times of crisis, even in a very efficient way. In circumstances like emergency cancellations, students can't expect all instructors to be terrific at online instruction; many teachers chose their profession because they love students, and value the in-person interaction in the classroom above all else. Teaching online is foreign and undesirable to many instructors, who are doing their best in less-than-ideal circumstances.

Adjusting your expectations to these realities as you get started will give you a better chance to earn the grades you want in your courses.

ORGANIZATION

Instructors organize their courses in the best way they know how, but those organizational strategies may not match up with other classes or with students' own preferences. Some instructors keep all their assignments, resources, and readings in systems like Google Classroom, Canvas, or Moodle. Others incorporate web functions like Facebook groups, Twitter, Google Docs, and a wide variety of other resources. Even for one course, this can be overwhelming. Add in a schedule of four to six courses, each individually planned by a different instructor with specific ideas about how a class should be created, and you have a potential mess.

And then we have course-related communication. Some instructors keep everything contained in course-defined systems; others use as many communication channels as are available. Some instructors send one long, multi-faceted message per week; others shoot out an announcement every time new information occurs to them.

Great online students don't rely on their instructors' organizational strategies to guide their work. They create their own organizational systems and integrate their online courses into them, so that they have a single calendar and digital workspace to store, complete, and review their work for all their courses. They keep communication organized in ways that allow them to track and remember the information provided by all their instructors. And they create a work environment—preferably physical, but digital if that's not possible—that allows them to treat their schoolwork in the online environment like a physical school with walls, desks, and lockers.

How organized are you? Check all the tools you like to use to keep your schoolwork organized:

☐ Printed planner   ☐ App calendar on phone

☐ Wall calendar   ☐ App calender on laptop

☐ School app system   ☐ Handwritten to-do list

☐ Other: _____   ☐ Other: _____

Which ones work best for you?

☐ Printed planner   ☐ App calendar on phone

☐ Wall calendar   ☐ App calender on laptop

☐ School app system   ☐ Handwritten to-do list

☐ Other: _____   ☐ Other: _____

TIME MANAGEMENT

Students who thrive in online courses organize their time well, along with their information and their workspaces. The number one reason my students fail to complete online courses is simply forgetting to do the work. Invariably, at the end of a semester, a handful of online students will write me to tell me they're sorry, but they simply forgot about our class. That's the hazard of online courses: no one might be taking attendance. No one is nagging you in-person to do your work. You have to make choices, and the choices you make are up to you. Good instructors do our best to reach out to students and keep them engaged, but without students making time for their work, instructors can only do so much.

Students who thrive keep a daily schedule that includes time allotted to every online class, even if they don't have work due or a specific activity scheduled by their instructor. They check in with their own progress on each course, make notes on that progress, and reflect on their successes and needs. They stick to their schedule on a daily basis, and schedule time off just as they would for in-person classes. They also make smart choices about their own time-related needs: Will a research essay take you longer online than it might if you were working in a library? Will reading online take longer than reading a printed handout or book (probably yes—more on that later)? Will you need to read twice on screen to get the full comprehension you would in a book (again, probably yes)? A daily schedule that accounts for both the regular work and the additional challenges of the online context allows you time and space to learn well and earn good grades.

How good are you at self-discipline and time management? Be honest! Name the things that help you stay focused and the things that cause you to waste time:

_____

_____

_____

_____

_____

_____

_____

STUDY SKILLS

Most of us learn study skills from an early age, but online classes test us. Yes, we know how to read. But do we know how to read well to learn? And do we choose to do so? Most important study skills involve organization and planning, but students also need to think about how effectively they read, what tools they use, and how they understand and engage with assignments and requirements in online classes, where students are responsible for understanding what they need to do without a teacher standing in front of them to repeat details and remind them of every expectation.

RESOURCEFULNESS

The internet is a bottomless well of resources. The trouble with the democratizing of information is that all information, valuable and less-so, is available in the same context. We don't always know where to find the good stuff, or what to ignore. This is the first principle of online research, a skill most of us don't master until college, if at all. But it's also important for online learning. What are the digital resources that help us thrive, in and out of class? Which ones hinder or distract us? How will we know?

Within an online class, you are likely to be provided with all the resources you need to complete your work. But as with course organization, those resources might not be arranged in ways that are most useful to your learning style or habits. And of course the resources for one class might overlap with or contradict those of another course.

The most prepared and successful online students spend time familiarizing themselves with and organizing their resources before they tackle coursework, finding new resources they might need, and asking good questions about those resources. Later, in the moment when resources are needed, they know exactly where to look to find answers and information.

List the resources you seek out when you need information:

_____

_____

_____

_____

ABOUT THIS BOOK

This book is your manual for successful online learning. Its sections will help you stay organized, attentive, and thoughtful in your studies. I'll provide specific and clear strategies for success so that you can make smart choices about your learning in any context.

The first section, Get it Together, explores ways to prepare yourself for the work of online courses as you get started. The second, Every Day, provides helpful ways of thinking about reading, communication, and other everyday tasks that are made more difficult in online learning situations. The third, Tools & Resources, is filled with guidance and templates for keeping track of everything along the way.

GET IT TOGETHER

YOUR DIGITAL CLASSROOM

When you can't go to a classroom to learn, you are best served by building your own. Your work will be more consistent, focused, and effective if you have some kind of dedicated learning space that you use consistently, every time you do classwork. That doesn't mean a home office! It doesn't even have to mean your own desk. It could be a particular chair at the kitchen table or a barstool at the counter where you devote yourself to creating and maintaining a consistent schedule and location.

What does that look like for you? That depends on your classes and materials. It might mean that you keep your notebook, calendar, and this workbook, along with your laptop or tablet in a particular place, and you carry them to your digital classroom. It might mean that you need more materials—a webcam, speakers, books, anything necessary for your classwork. You might choose to keep all your materials in a box or binder close to your workspace. Maybe you *do* have a desk, or even an area that can become your home office. If so, while you're doing your classwork, make sure it's free of anything you're *not* using for classes. Just like we minimize distractions on the screen to the best of our ability while we read (more on that later), we should minimize distractions in our space while we work.

Describe the spot where you do your schoolwork at home. Try to include at least one detail from each of your five senses (sight, sound, touch, taste, smell):

_____

_____

_____

_____

_____

_____

_____

_____

_____

_____

_____

_____

_____

It even means that our pens, scrap paper, and highlighters, or any other tools we use, are set aside, used *only* for classwork during our digital work time. Your laptop or tablet should be as cleared of distractions as possible, too: close your messaging app, your personal email, and any tabs in your browser that aren't directly related to your classwork. (Close the social media apps. All of them. Keep them closed. I promise this will help.) The one exception to this guideline is music: many students actually study *more* effectively with music playing, so if that's you, here's your permission to keep your music player open. But even in that case, have control of that aspect of your environment: make a few playlists you know will help you concentrate instead of distracting you, and have those at the ready on your phone, tablet, or laptop when you sit down to work. Even think about your speakers or headphones. I don't work well, for example, with music blaring at me from my laptop speakers or with headphones on, so I bought a cheap-but-loud Bluetooth mini-speaker that I keep on the other side of the room while I work.

We can't always clear all the distractions away from our workspace, of course. If you have children or younger siblings, they're likely to burst in and interrupt. Your pets may demand your attention. A delivery might interrupt you. We can't control every aspect of the world around us. But you will give yourself the best chance of focusing and learning effectively if you control as much of your environment as you possibly can.

Use the list on page 61 to catalogue all the items you can think of that you'll need for your classes. Be as detailed as possible. If those items (like a shared family computer) cannot be stored with the rest of your work

What do you love about the space where you do your schoolwork? What do you hate about it? What do you wish it had more of? Less of?

materials, make a note of where they're usually located and who else uses them so that you can always find them before your work time begins.

Use the list on page 62 to clear your physical and digital study spaces each time you sit down to work. List everything that gets in the way of your concentration, both on and off the screen, and take a couple of minutes before your work time to get rid of all of it.

YOUR DIGITAL WORKDAY

Just like your space, you want to make the time you spend on your classes as consistent and controlled as possible. Most students underestimate the amount of time they'll need to devote to online classes, but when you plan ahead, you can give yourself plenty of time to do great work.

Start by considering how much time you'd be spending on a class if it were in-person. If you're in college, the general guideline is two to three hours of non-class study time per hour in the classroom, so three to four hours per week per credit hour. For a three-hour course, that's nine to 12 hours per week. If you're enrolled in 15 credit hours, you should plan to spend 45-60 hours per week on your coursework. That's a lot! For most students, some classes will require the full nine-12 hours per week, or even more, and some will require much less. The time you budget should also depend on your familiarity with the subject. If you're taking an elective in an area you know nothing about, plan to put some time into familiarizing yourself with basic background information; for a course that builds on a subject you've been studying for a while, you may not need this extra time. When you do this math, you can see why 12 hours is a full-time courseload! If you're working, parenting, managing a social or family life, or even just thinking about how to take the best care of yourself, managing your classwork efficiently is vital.

If you're taking 15 hours of classes and doing *anything* else, will it be

How much time do you usually spend on schoolwork at home? Do you feel rushed? Do you feel like you can slow down? What would make your work time better?

_____

_____

_____

_____

_____

_____

_____

_____

_____

_____

_____

_____

_____

possible to carve out 60 hours to devote to nothing but coursework per week, every week? Probably not. But it's a good idea to start from there and move backwards toward a more realistic expectation. Planning your week based on the time you realistically might need, rather than on the time you have available, is one key to succeeding in any class, but especially online courses you'll be tempted to ignore when life gets busy. Once you have your course syllabi, you can take a look at your professors' expectations and create an estimate of how much of the suggested time you'll really need. This requires some self-knowledge and experience, but if you estimate a bit high, you'll end up in great shape.

If you're a high school or middle school student engaging in online learning, you'll need a slightly different approach to estimating your time. If you're able to devote the exact amount of time to an online class that you would usually spend in the classroom, plus the amount you would spend on homework, as long as you're organized, you'll be in good shape. It may be helpful to add in time to deal with the online interface, particularly if your school is using online learning in an emergency circumstance or is inexperienced with online education.

The most important aspect of scheduling is planning to devote enough time to your studies. The second most important aspect is consistency. You will do your best work if you do it at the same time, on the same schedule, every week. Once you know how much time you will need, your next step is to take an honest look at your schedule, including any work, household, and family obligations. Write everything down in whatever type of calendar or planner you prefer, or enter it into your digital calendar. Add any occasions you'll need to account for, like holidays or family plans. Write down daily or weekly schedule aspects like the comings and goings of family members or

What things do you do while you're completing schoolwork that are not schoolwork, like snacks, TV, etc? Which of those things help you stay focused? Which distract?

_____

_____

_____

_____

_____

_____

_____

_____

_____

_____

_____

_____

_____

roommates. Then consider what times of day and week you can best schedule your work. If your classes are not all digital, you'll of course have to work around days and times when you'll attend school. If your online courses are synchronous, meaning you have specific times when you have to log into your courses, you'll obviously use that time for a portion of your work. But if your classes are all asynchronous and online, you will have to make choices about when you'll do your best work, schedule that time, and stick to it. Treat your online work time the same way you would treat a job. Schedule yourself for a shift every day, plan which classwork you'll do during that shift, and show up for yourself every time. Use the Calculating Your Worktime worksheet on page 63 and the sample weekly and daily schedules on pages 65-66 as models, or create your own if you have a preferred way of doing so.

ORGANIZING YOUR COURSES

Here's the situation: You have four to six courses at once. You want to do your best in *all* of them. But when you log into your digital course management platform, you feel immediately overwhelmed. One class is organized in a way that makes perfect sense to your learning style and preferences. One is simple a holding pen for PDFs that stand in for printed handouts your teacher would use in the classroom, with few or no interactive elements. Another teacher has loaded every reading, activity and expectation into the platform's calendar, which is now cluttered and useless. One course is organized by assignment, another by course unit, another by week. Yet another course is full of links to outside resources and instructions to use other platforms for some tasks, with only minimal use of the primary platform.

For you, the student, this is a big mess. Each time you log in, you have to shift into four to six different learning styles to navigate your classes. The struggle to deal with these shifts is one of the biggest reasons students don't complete online courses: the frustration multiplies as a course unfolds, and students simply give up.

The key to managing a mess is always to clean it up. So how do you clean up your courses? You create your own organizational scaffold, likely on your

Check all the places you go to find information about your classes and to complete assignments:

- ☐ Printed syllabus
- ☐ Canvas or Blackboard
- ☐ Google Classroom
- ☐ Social media
- ☐ Class site or blog
- ☐ Personal planner/notebook
- ☐ Other: _____
- ☐ Other: _____

What devices and tools do you use?

- ☐ Printed planner
- ☐ Smartphone
- ☐ Tablet
- ☐ Laptop or desktop
- ☐ Notebook
- ☐ Pens, pencils, highligters
- ☐ Headphones/speakers
- ☐ Stylus for tablet screen
- ☐ Lapdesk
- ☐ Other: _____

laptop or tablet, that allows you to stay on top of the varied interfaces and expectations scattered across your digital learning platform(s).

Check out the scaffolding templates on pages 67-69, pick and choose their approaches, or create your own. The most important aspect of organizing your learning materials is that you are comfortable with your approach and can engage it consistently in the same way, day after day.

What organizational tools would you like to have? Which might make completing your classwork easier or more comfortable? Can you imagine ways to get those things?

EVERY DAY

COMMUNICATION STRATEGIES

Many professors who teach online include policies about "netiquette," meaning ways to communicate appropriately in digital environments. For many reasons, digital communication can be misunderstood and mismanaged. Tone is easily lost in written contexts, especially when those writing aren't experts. Simple errors caused by distraction, tiredness, or just plain accidents can result in miscommunication. Likewise, reading on a screen (see the next section!) is a ripe environment for missed information. Further, our attitudes about online communication have been forever shaped by social media and review platforms like Yelp and Rate My Professor, which encourage anonymous reviewers to write things they would *never* say if they had to take responsibility for their words. It's difficult to remember that a class context should feel much more like a professional environment than a Twitter thread.

Good communication has two components— sending and receiving—and each is made up of both content and form. That is, what you say and how you say it, and what is said and how you receive it. All four of those elements require extra care and consideration in online learning environments, where the vast majority of communication is

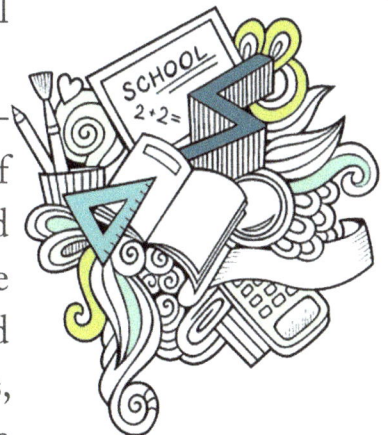

How many school-related emails do you receive in a day?

_____

How many in a week?

_____

How many school-related texts or other types of message besides email do you receive in a day? In a week?

_____

How many school-related emails do you send in a day? In a week?

_____

How many school-related texts or other types of message besides email do you send in a day? In a week?

_____

How many of each do you think you *need* to send or receive?

_____

_____

written rather than spoken, conveyed without the immediate opportunity for clarification, and subject to whatever stresses, distractions, and moods might dominate your teachers' and peers' home environments. Some general guidelines can help. First, when you're writing or creating a message for class:

To the very best of your ability, use accurate grammar and spelling, complete sentences, and clear language choices. This conveys your professionalism, of course, but it also reduces the likelihood that you'll be misunderstood.

Take the time to plan out your message, whether that message will be delivered via email, chat, discussion board, or comment. That's more difficult in a live chat context, but otherwise, you should never rush to put information out into your class channels.

Explain yourself fully. Never assume your message's recipient knows or remembers the context of your question, comment, or idea. Your professor and peers can always skim past any extraneous information.

When asking a question, do your very best to find an answer on your own first. Your teachers have dozens, possibly hundreds of students and, while they love (or should love) to help you, sorting through simple, unnecessary questions that can be answered with a quick skim of the syllabus and schedule ("When is this project due?") slows down vital work like grading, answering substantive questions, and preparing lessons for you. If you find an answer but need more information, make it clear to your teacher that you looked and need more detail, so your teacher knows that you made the effort.

Do what you can to keep your communications to a minimum. It's easy to be overwhelmed by the amount of email, in particular, involved in online education, so if you have more than one non-timely question, keep track of them in your notebook and send them all at once rather than shooting off a message every time a question or idea occurs to you (and hope that your teachers and classmates do the same).

And when you're receiving information:

Assume goodness. If there are two ways to read an instruction, email, chat comment, or other communiqué, choose the most generous possible interpretation. You, of course, are now equipped to make great choices when you send a message, but keep in mind that everyone is probably overwhelmed by the sheer amount of communication and not everyone will do as great a job as you. Your teachers might have upwards of fifty emails per day to answer, and might read too fast or dash off a reply too quickly. (We hope not, but nobody's perfect, and we don't have the right to expect them to be!) And when we're online for emergency purposes like school cancellations, teachers and students alike might be handling childcare, family concerns, and other distractions while working. Do everything in your power to be patient and kind.

Don't expect instant replies. Your teachers and peers might need a day or more to get back to you, and will appreciate your patience.

Consolidate the messages you receive, as well as those you send. In a perfect world, your teachers and peers would take the same consideration as you to avoid bombarding everyone with messages, but that's not always what happens. You'll have more information at hand if you keep messages in a

"Netiquette" is a made-up word describing our approach to professionalism in digital communication. Describe how you currently choose tone, style, and content in your school-related communication:

_____

_____

_____

_____

_____

_____

_____

_____

_____

_____

_____

_____

folder grouped by class, and perhaps by topic, to review in a timely fashion, rather than reading them as they roll in and then promptly forgetting their content.

Consider keeping a log of important information you receive, including taking notes on your course organization worksheets of all relevant information and updates to assignments as you read and review incoming information. Try the sample below.

COMMUNICATION LOG

Class: _____

Date: _____ Type of Communication: (email, etc.) _____

From: _____

Subject/summary: _____

_____

_____

_____

☐ Recorded/changed in calendar/schedule if needed?

☐ Recorded/changed in Assignment Worksheet?

Check all the communication methods currently required for your schoolwork:

☐ Email

☐ Discussion Board

☐ Full class chat

☐ Social media closed group

☐ Blog posts

☐ Texting

☐ Streaming sessions

☐ Small group chat

☐ Public social media posts

☐ Other: _____

The tips below can keep your communication clear and effective. Also check out the Communication Checklists in Tools & Resources.

EMAIL

- **Treat emails you send like a formal letter,** not a text message or conversation. Always use an appropriate greeting (Dear Professor X:) and salutation (Yours truly, You), and format your email in clear paragraphs rather than a big block of text. Keep your paragraphs short, and use academically appropriate grammar, spelling, and punctuation. Remember that email is official communication that will stay in your teacher's record of your work and, should any later conflicts arise, may be passed to officials in your school or university as evidence of your performance in class. Treat emails as the official documents they are.

- If you need to reveal private information to your professor that you do not wish to have included in your academic record, use email to ask for a phone or video conference, if those are available. Understand that your teacher may not be at liberty to speak with you off the record, but ask anyway.

- Be extra careful with "reply" vs. "reply-all" functions. There is almost never a good reason to use "reply-all," so avoid it if at all possible. In most cases, it adds unnecessary work for everyone to deal with.

- As with everything you read on screen, read email messages carefully, all the way through, and take notes where notes might be helpful.

GROUP CHAT

- Group chats move quickly, so it's difficult to plan ahead, but a great rule is to never say anything in a group chat that you wouldn't say in an in-person class discussion.

- Stay on topic. Unlike an in-person class discussion, group chats are recorded, so they become part of the class record. Stick to the prompts at hand.

- Before you enter a chat designed to cover a reading assignment or to serve as a study session for an exam, prepare three clear, specific questions to share with your classmates. Write them down in your notes in order of importance to your own understanding of the class material. When your teacher opens the chat up for discussion, share them one at a time. If your teacher asks for responses to a specific prompt, don't derail with your questions, but participate in the prompt.

- Interact with your classmates, not just your teacher. Group chats are meant to be *group* chats, not one-on-one conversations with a teacher in front of everyone else. (Think about how annoying it is when that happens in class. No fun.)

In whatever way your interface allows, save the group chat for your notes/files. You might be able to copy/paste into a document, print to PDF, or simply save the whole thing. Label your file with the date, time, and if possible, topic ("10-23-20—Exam 3 Study Session").

DISCUSSION BOARDS

Stay on topic. As with group chats, discussion threads are designed to accomplish a specific learning purpose, whether that purpose is clear to you or not.

Don't just drop your post and run. That's not a discussion. Good discussion board participation involves everyone commenting on everyone else's sub-threads and exchanging ideas and responses, so make sure you reply to your classmates and engage with their replies to you.

For the first few uses of discussion boards, take a look at the time stamps on your classmates' contributions and try to participate around that time if you can. You might not be able to, but being digitally present and participatory in the thick of the activity will help you generate ideas and develop your own thinking.

Follow directions closely when they're provided, especially if the discussion board will be graded. As with all written communication, discussion boards are part of the permanent record of the class. Plan your individual contributions ahead of time, including drafting and spell-checking them if you can, and use academically appropriate grammar, spelling, and punctuation.

STREAMING/ZOOM SESSIONS

- ❧ Ask your teacher to record and share the session so that you may have it to review later.

- ❧ Be sure to find out ahead of time if a streaming session is designed to be a lecture/demonstration or a discussion. If you're expected to participate in discussion, prepare as you would for a group chat, writing three points of discussion ahead of time to bring to the session. If the session is a lecture or demonstration, have all your materials ready to take robust notes so that you'll be ready to jump right in.

- ❧ In your notes, identify anything you write down by time and speaker, so you can skip ahead to that point in the recording if you need to review later. For example, if the session starts at 2:00 p.m. and someone explains an important concept at 2:14 p.m., write "14 minutes" in the margin next to those notes and who was speaking, so you can easily revisit that detail later without having to watch the full recording. Try the template on page 72 for starters.

READING ONLINE

When we read on a screen, our reading comprehension decreases. The reasons for this include distraction on the live web, our tendency to skim when we scroll, and our physiological response to the lighted screen, which means the causes are both shallow and deep; they encompass the entire process of reading.

This is true, of course, for face-to-face classwork as well. Instructors have been sharing ditigal handouts and providing electronic textbooks for years. But in most cases, students, teachers, and families choose paper texts for reading that requires deep comprehension. I recommend that my students consider printing digital material if they struggle to read on screen, but of course that's an expensive solution that's not great for our environment, and only solves *some* of the problem.

In digital learning, however, all materials, from course information to project instructions to reading assignments are delivered online, often in formats that don't lend well to printing even if students want to. This means that every step of an online course requires students to overcome the substantial challenges presented by the screen, despite the convenience of inserting annotations and searching a text.

Reflect on your own reading process: Do you feel you learn best reading a printed page? Or on a screen? Why?

_____

_____

_____

_____

_____

Test yourself: Find full-text pages of school-related material. Read one page on screen. Print and read another. Compare those experiences. Was one faster? Did you retain information better from one than the other?

_____

_____

_____

_____

_____

Are you a person who likes to read, or hates to read? Do you know why?

_____

_____

_____

_____

_____

_____

Test yourself: Find two more pages to read, one on screen and one in print. Take handwritten notes from each. How did that affect your experience? Your comprehension?

_____

_____

_____

_____

_____

_____

Here's what we know, based on research:

- Reading on screen on a live website is the least effective way to learn and comprehend. Distractions from ads, images, links, and other temptations combine with our natural tendency to skim on lighted screens to reduce our focus. Plus, lighted screens cause eye fatigue much more quickly than printed pages or e-ink readers like Kindles.

- Reading a PDF or other non-web text on a screen is one step better; it reduces the number of distractions, but still falls into the trap of skimming and causes eye fatigue.

- Using an e-ink reader like a Kindle for electronic textbooks helps eliminate distractions and some of the eye fatigue, but still doesn't help with our tendency to skim on screens of all kinds.

Only one approach has been proven to mitigate the negative impacts of reading on screen: taking notes with a pen on paper. Note taking on a laptop or tablet can be helpful, and it's easier to keep those notes organized and available, but they don't solve the problem of reading on screen, and as an added difficulty, they replicate those problems when you open your device to study them later. So: paper and pens it is. Or should be. Even better, taking notes in your own handwriting on paper is a bit of a magic trick: the act of writing those notes down serves to help teach yourself the material so that you may not even need to review it later. It also activates an area of your brain that typing does not, resulting in a more fully integrated thinking process while you learn. Even if it's possible to copy and paste the material you're studying into a note-taking app, recreate the notes yourself. Remember, your goal is engaged learning, not an easier, faster process.

Some learners cannot take notes this way, of course, due to a disability. If that's you, make sure you contact your school's disability services staff to maximize your access to learning. They exist entirely to facilitate an equitable learning experience for you, and are required by law to help you, so take advantage of their services.

Try out the note-taking template on page 73 as one good way to organize your notes, or use another organization if you like. You can always use a digtial method, but keep in mind that handwritten notes have proven to be the most effective way to learn and retain what you read.

ACTIVE LEARNING

You're sitting in class and your mind wanders. What happens? Your teacher or professor calls your attention back. Or you realize you were spacing out and ask enough questions to catch up. Online? That doesn't happen. You have to manage your attention yourself. All the devices we use to study online introduce distractions, but you can't just put them away like you might choose—or be required—to do in a classroom. Your learning in an online class has to be active at all times. That requires knowing yourself really well, and understanding what affects your ability to pay attention. On top of that, students often don't pay close attention to online materials, under the assumption that they can just look them over later, though most never do.

One foolproof way to maximize our attention, and then to spend less time reviewing material, is to take notes as a habit, not in order to study them later, or because you think you'll need to review, but because the act of taking notes, especially by hand, activates your brain in engagement with the material, as you read in Reading Online. If you make it part of your learning practice *every time* you do your schoolwork, it will also give you a solid, predictable base of activity that's part of your learning process. We know that some students learn better by reading, some from videos, some

Think about your attention span for classwork. How long can you sit still without needing to get up and move?

_____

What snacks, drinks, and activities refresh you best?

_____

_____

_____

What types of learning activities or study practices make you feel tired the most quickly?

_____

_____

_____

_____

_____

from visual learning tools. But if your note-taking practice is the same for all kinds of course materials, you'll have a stable base for your active learning practice, whatever form your lessons come in.

A few other practices will help you maximize your understanding and benefit from any type of teaching. While these represent a bit of extra work, you can consider them a trade-off for the time saved in not going to your school or campus:

- Ask your instructor to record and post any and all video or meeting sessions for later review. This will help decrease the sense of urgency that you have to take in every single detail of a discussion or lecture on the spot.

- Begin each learning session, no matter its format, with goals and questions in mind. Where possible, actively participate in any discussion or meeting sessions during their most active times to increase engagement and response, and keep track of your work as well as the ideas shared by others.

- Plan breaks every 30 to 50 minutes, based on what you think feels best for your mind and body, and whenever possible, use those breaks to move around, stretch, perhaps even take a 10-minute walk or complete another task that uses your body more than your mind, like starting a load of laundry. If physical activity is not possible or helpful for you, at least rest your eyes away from screens. Snack breaks are great, too, as long as you pay attention to your physical needs and don't just eat because you're bored.

- Take loads of notes using the templates in Tools & Resources or The Digital Undergrad Notebook.

TOOLS & RESOURCES

TEMPLATES AND GUIDES

The following pages are made up of checklists, templates, guides, and samples for all your study, note-taking, and communication practices.

ORGANIZING YOUR SPACE:

    YOUR PERFECT WORKSPACE: STUFF YOU NEED

    YOUR PERFECT WORKSPACE: STUFF TO REMOVE

ORGANIZING YOUR TIME:

    CALCULATING YOUR WORK TIME

    DAILY ONLINE STUDY SCHEDULE

    WEEKLY ONLINE STUDY SCHEDULE

ORGANIZING YOUR COURSES: TEMPLATES

    PROJECT/TOPIC/UNIT COURSE ORGANIZATION

    EXAM-BASED COURSE ORGANIZATION

    WEEKLY CALENDAR COURSE ORGANIZATION

UNDERSTANDING ASSIGNMENTS WORKSHEET

NOTE-TAKING TEMPLATES:

LECTURE NOTES

VIDEO/STREAMING SESSION NOTES

READING ASSIGNMENT NOTES

COMMUNICATION CHECKLISTS:

EMAIL

GROUP CHAT POST

DICSUSSON BOARD PARTICIPATION

ASSIGNMENT CHECKLIST: BEFORE YOU SUBMIT WORK

APPS, SITES, AND LOGINS

ADDITIONAL NOTES PAGES

YOUR PERFECT WORKSPACE INCLUDES:

Every time you sit down to work, check off your customized version of this list:

- ☐ Laptop or tablet
- ☐ Notebooks
- ☐ Highlighters
- ☐ Headphones/speakers
- ☐ Other: _____

- ☐ Planner
- ☐ Pens/Pencils/stylus
- ☐ Smartphone
- ☐ Lapdesk
- ☐ Other: _____

Reminder: Where to find everything

Item	Shared	Mine	Where is it?
Laptop or Tablet	☐	☐	_____
Notebooks	☐	☐	_____
Pens, pencils, etc.	☐	☐	_____
Headphones/speakers	☐	☐	_____
Planner	☐	☐	_____
Stylus	☐	☐	_____
Smartphone	☐	☐	_____
Lapdesk	☐	☐	_____
Other: _____	☐	☐	_____

YOUR PERFECT WORKSPACE DOES NOT INCLUDE:

Get rid of all the stuff that distracts you each time you sit down to do schoolwork by checking off your customized version of this list:

- ☐ Headphones or speakers if music distracts you

- ☐ Friends, siblings, children, people

- ☐ Turn off the TV

- ☐ Close social media apps

- ☐ Close texting/messaging apps if possible

- ☐ Eat, then clear away dishes/snack wrappers/etc.

- ☐ Remove empty cups or water bottles, or fill them

- ☐ Clear away clutter, art supplies, etc.

- ☐ Wash your hands, and your face if you haven't today

- ☐ Other: _____

- ☐ Other: _____

CALCULATING YOUR WORK TIME: COLLEGE STUDENTS

This page is designed to help you determine how much time you need for your online study week.

For every credit hour a college student spends in class, that student is expected to spend 3-4 studying out of the classroom, with variation for specialized classes and levels of preparedness. Most college students don't report spending quite this much time on their school work, though certainly those with extra challenges or difficult majors should plan to. To figure expected time, do this:

Number of credit hours enrolled: 12

4 study hours per credit: 48

Adjust to accommodate for ease or difficulty: 36 to 42 hours

It will also be helpful to break that down by class:

3 credit English class, lots of reading and writing: 12 hrs/week

3 credit Spanish class, mostly workbook & practice: 6 hrs/week

3 credit History class, tons of reading & writing: 10 hrs/week

3 credit math class, math is difficult for me: 12 hrs/week

For a total of 40 study hours each week.

CALCULATING YOUR WORK TIME: HIGH SCHOOL

This page is designed to help you determine how much time you need for your online study week.

High school students spend roughly six hours per day in class and 18 hours on homework each week in face-to-face school settings, for a total of 48 hours per week. That's a heavy work load! Students moving to an online routine should be honest about the amount of time they actually spend studying and work hard to be as efficient as possible. To figure expected time, you have two choices:

Number of hours normally spent in classes each week: 30

Hours typically spent on homework: 18

Adjust based on experience and preparedness: 36 to 42 hours

Or you may wish to consider what your actual classes will look like, since most K-12 schools set out specific guidelines:

Actual synchronous time announced to be required per week (for streaming sessions or time required to be logged into school apps): 25 hours

Estimate of homework time based on actual assignments: 10 hours/week.

For a total of 35 study hours each week.

DAILY ONLINE STUDY SCHEDULE

This layout is a sample for a schedule of four online classes. You can create your own schedule or agenda based on your authentic time needs after using the Calculating Your Work Time worksheet on the previous pages.

Mondays	
10:00	Organize my space
10:10–11:00	Log in; work on English
11:00	Break, short walk
11:10–12:00	Log in; work on History
12:00–12:30	Lunch
12:30–2:00	Log in; Work on Calculus
2:00–2:50	Spanish Class Zoom
2:50–3:00	Break; small snack
3:00–3:50	Read book for English class

WEEKLY ONLINE STUDY SCHEDULE

This layout is for a schedule of four online classes. You can create your own schedule based on your authentic time needs after using the Calculating Your Work Time worksheet on the previous pages. This schedule functions like a structured to-do list; this method may work best if your classes are built around projects and exams—work that comes in bursts—rather than daily study. Some weeks on such a schedule might be more full than others.

Monday	Tuesday	Wednesday	Thursday	Friday
Organize my space	Organize my space	Organize my space	Organize my space	Organize my space
Watch video for History	Spanish Class Zoom (9 am)	Math Test (2 hours)	Draft English Essay (2 hrs)	History Zoom (9 am)
(break)	(break)	(break)	(break)	(break)
Study for math test (2 hours)	Work on English Paper (2 hours)	History Homework (1.5 hours)	Draft English Essay (2 hrs)	Work on paper for History (2 hours)
Lunch	Lunch	Lunch	Lunch	Lunch
Find sources for English Essay (3 hours)	Read articles for History (2 hours)	Spanish Homework (2 hours)	Math Homework (1 hour)	Spanish Homework (2 hours)
	Study for Math test (1 hour)	Reading for English (2 hours)	Spanish Video (2 hours)	Proofread English Essay

PROJECT/TOPIC/UNIT CLASS ORGANIZATION

Your professors or teachers will each organize classes in the way that makes the most sense to them and that fits most closely with the course's learning objectives. But that may not be the way that makes the most sense to you, and coordinating multiple mismatched course structures can be overwhelming. If your classes make the most sense to you when organized by subject, topic, or unit, use this template to combine them all into one learning plan. Fun tip: color-code your classes to make it more visually appealing and easier to read. (Your version will likely be several pages long.)

Project 1: [title] _____
   Class: _____
   Format: [paper/visual project/exam/etc.] _____
   Due Date: _____ Group Members: [names & contact info]
How much of final grade does this count for? [points and percentage]

Project 2: [title] _____
   Class: _____
   Format: [paper/visual project/exam/etc.] _____
   Due Date: _____ Group Members: [names & contact info]
How much of final grade does this count for? [points and percentage]

Project 3: [title] _____
   Class: _____
   Format: [paper/visual project/exam/etc.] _____
   Due Date: _____ Group Members: [names & contact info]
How much of final grade does this count for? [points and percentage]

Project 4: [title] _____
   Class: _____
   Format: [paper/visual project/exam/etc.] _____
   Due Date: _____ Group Members: [names & contact info]
How much of final grade does this count for? [points and percentage]

EXAM-BASED COURSE ORGANIZATION

Your professors or teachers will each organize classes in the way that makes the most sense to them and that fits most closely with the course's learning objectives. But that may not be the way that makes the most sense to you, and coordinating multiple mismatched course structures can be overwhelming. If your classes make the most sense to you when organized around exams that punctuate a term, this template can help get your information all in one place. Fun tip: color-code your classes to make it more visually appealing and easier to read. (Your version will likely be several pages long.)

Exam 1: [class & unit] _____

    Subject: [topics and sub-topics; pages to study, etc.] _____

    Exam Date: _____ Study Session date: _____

    How much of final grade does this count for? [points and percentage]

Exam 2: [class & unit] _____

    Subject: [topics and sub-topics; pages to study, etc.] _____

    Exam Date: _____ Study Session date: _____

    How much of final grade does this count for? [points and percentage]

Exam 3: [class & unit] _____

    Subject: [topics and sub-topics; pages to study, etc.] _____

    Exam Date: _____ Study Session date: _____

    How much of final grade does this count for? [points and percentage]

Exam 4: [class & unit] _____

    Subject: [topics and sub-topics; pages to study, etc.] _____

    Exam Date: _____ Study Session date: _____

    How much of final grade does this count for? [points and percentage]

Exam 5: [class & unit] _____

    Subject: [topics and sub-topics; pages to study, etc.] _____

    Exam Date: _____ Study Session date: _____

    How much of final grade does this count for? [points and percentage]

WEEKLY CALENDAR COURSE ORGANIZATION

Your professors or teachers will each organize classes in the way that makes the most sense to them and that fits most closely with the course's learning objectives. But that may not be the way that makes the most sense to you, and coordinating multiple mismatched course structures can be overwhelming. If your classes make the most sense to you when organized around a weekly calendar, use this template to bring all your materials together. Fun tip: color-code your classes to make it more visually appealing and easier to read. (Your version will likely be several pages long.)

Week 1: [dates]

Class: [title] _____ Virtual meetings or chats: [dates, times & formats] _____
Assignments: _____
Resources: [links or lists of locations] _____

Class: [title] _____ Virtual meetings or chats: [dates, times & formats] _____
Assignments: _____
Resources: [links or lists of locations] _____

Class: [title] _____ Virtual meetings or chats: [dates, times & formats] _____
Assignments: _____
Resources: [links or lists of locations] _____

Class: [title] _____ Virtual meetings or chats: [dates, times & formats] _____
Assignments: _____
Resources: [links or lists of locations] _____

Week 2: [dates]

Class: [title] _____ Virtual meetings or chats: [dates, times & formats] _____
Assignments: _____
Resources: [links or lists of locations] _____

UNDERSTANDING ASSIGNMENTS: A WORKSHEET

However your instructor provides or structures expectations and instructions, you can standardize your approach with this worksheet so that you know everything you need to know and have everything available at a glance.

Title: _____ Format: *(paper/exam/portfolio/etc.)*

Due Date(s): _____ Required Components: *(if an assignment contains multiple steps, activities, or documents, list them here and complete a separate worksheet for each of them)*

Part of: *[Larger assignment, unit, or assignment group here]*

Important dates: *[any draft due dates, study sessions, or components that are due before the final due date here]*

Length or depth requirements: *[pages, sources, formats for a paper; number of questions and style of questions for an exam; number of sub-assignments for a packet or portfolio; components of a visual project listed here]*

What am I supposed to learn from this? _____

What should I already know as I begin this? _____

How does this apply to other work we'll do in class or in other classes?

_____

How much time am I expected to spend on this? _____

What questions do I have for my professor/teacher? _____

_____

Professor's answers: _____

_____

LECTURE NOTES TEMPLATE

Class   Date   Topic, if applicable   Lecturer Name

Preparation: (any readings or homework on the agenda)

_____

Notes:
 (Time—Subject)

_____

_____

_____

_____

(Time—Subject)

_____

_____

_____

Summary of Lecture:

_____

_____

_____

Questions for follow-up:

_____

_____

VIDEO/STREAMING CLASS MEETING NOTES TEMPLATE

Class   Date   Title, if applicable   Session Leader

Preparation: (any readings or homework on the agenda)

_____

Questions for Discussion:

_____

_____

Notes:
 (Time—Speaker)

_____

_____

 (Time—Speaker)

_____

_____

Summary of Discussion:

_____

_____

Questions for follow-up:

_____

_____

_____

READING ASSIGNMENTS NOTES TEMPLATE

Class   Date   Title   Author

Summary: _____

_____

_____

_____

_____

_____

_____

_____

_____

Questions for Discussion: _____

_____

_____

_____

How it relates to class unit/assignment: _____

_____

_____

_____

_____

_____

_____

_____

EMAIL CHECKLIST

Remember that emails sent within your class context are professional documents and may become part of your academic record in any case where a conflict about grades, policies, or interpersonal communciations arise. Treat them with extra care. This checklist will help you do so; use it every time you prepare to send an email message.

- [ ] I have looked at the syllabus and assignment to make sure I couldn't answer my own question.

- [ ] I have fully explained my question and the reasons for it, and if necessary, have explained the steps I took to attempt to answer the question on my own before writing.

- [ ] I have reminded my teacher/professor which section of their class I am in and what project I'm working on, including my topic.

- [ ] If this is a reply, I have made the kindest and most generous possible interpretation of the message I'm replying to.

- [ ] If this is a reply, I have only selected "reply," not "reply-all," unless this is one of the rare circumstances where "reply-all" is absolutely necessary.

- [ ] I have addressed my professor or teacher by their proper or preferred name and title, and used an appropriate salutation.

- [ ] I have proofread my message for correctness.

GROUP CHAT POST CHECKLIST

Group chats, whether small-group or full-class, move quickly and can create anxiety. But before you post, remember that your posts are basically public and your classmates, even if they aren't posting, may be watching closely. Take care to prioritize others' voices as well as your own, and refrain from dominating a discussion, but do contribute carefully. Consider using the following checklist for each post you contribute:

- [ ] I have done the preparation necessary to participate in the group chat, including any reading or homework, before writing a post.

- [ ] My comment or question is directly relevant to the discussion and has not already been said by someone else.

- [ ] If possible, my question or comment invites others into the discussion, by name where appropriate. (Ex.: "Tara mentioned X. Can we talk more about [this aspect of] X?"

- [ ] I have done the work to find something valuable to say, instead of just posting to be sure my voice is heard.

- [ ] I am posting in a way that involves the whole group and not just my teacher.

- [ ] I would say this out loud in a public space or large lecture class, and would not mind it appearing in my academic record.

- [ ] What I am posting is kind, helpful, and thoughtful, allowing others to assume good intentions on my part.

DISCUSSION BOARD PARTICIPATION CHECKLIST

Discussion boards only work well if they generate actual discussion. Plan to engage as fully as possible with your classmates in them, replying meaningfully to their posts and engaging their replies on your posts. Be sure, as well, to stay on topic and follow any directions your professor or teacher has provided. And as with all other written communication, remember that your posts carry the possibility of becoming part of your academic record.

- [ ] To the best of my ability, I am participating in the discussion board at its busiest time to maximize interaction.

- [ ] My post is contributing something meaningful to the discussion. If others have posted, I am definitely not just repeating what they already said—I am adding something new.

- [ ] My post follows my professor's directions and accomplishes any stated discussion goals.

- [ ] I have done the preparation necessary to participate in the discussion, including reading or homework, before writing a post.

- [ ] I am posting in a way that invites conversation among my classmates and not just addressing my teacher.

- [ ] I would say this out loud in a public space or large lecture class, and would not mind it appearing in my academic record.

- [ ] What I am posting is kind, helpful, and thoughtful, allowing others to assume good intentions on my part.

- [ ] If I am replying to someone, I have assumed goodness about their post.

ASSIGNMENT CHECKLIST: BEFORE YOU SUBMIT WORK

When we take a class in person, we usually have a chance to ask a last set of questions before an exam or assignment is due. Not all online courses include that feature. Use this checklist at least a full business day before a due date to make sure you'll be in great shape.

- [ ] I have double-checked the assignment's full instructions and due date, and made sure my work fulfills the requirements.

- [ ] I have asked all my questions about the assignment in a reasonable time frame, knowing that my professor might not get back to me for 24-48 hours.

- [ ] I have made sure my work conforms to formatting, length, and file type requirements before attempting to submit.

- [ ] I know where to log in to submit the assignment or complete the test.

- [ ] I have consulted with any group or team members in advance of due dates to make sure we have our submission plans coordinated.

- [ ] I have asked for an extension within the required time frame if extensions are available and I think I might need one. I have double-checked the syllabus to make sure I have those details right.

- [ ] I have compiled all required pre-writing or prep documents and shown my work where necessary.

APPS, SITES, & LOGINS

One of the most frustrating aspects of online coursework is the overwhelming number of apps, web platforms, and logins students have to keep straight. Here's a worksheet for keeping track of it all, though you'll probably want yours to be digital so you can make direct links or copy URLs into your browser.

Site or App: _____ Needed for: (class or purpose)

Username: _____ Password: _____

Site or App: _____ Needed for: (class or purpose)

Username: _____ Password: _____

Site or App: _____ Needed for: (class or purpose)

Username: _____ Password: _____

Site or App: _____ Needed for: (class or purpose)

Username: _____ Password: _____

Site or App: _____ Needed for: (class or purpose)

Username: _____ Password: _____

Additional Notes:

_____

_____

_____

_____

_____

_____

_____

_____

_____

_____

_____

_____

_____

_____

_____

_____

_____

Additional Notes:

www.ingramcontent.com/pod-product-compliance
Lightning Source LLC
Chambersburg PA
CBHW061415090426
42742CB00024B/3472